# A Chorus of Frogs

## THE RISKY LIFE OF AN ANCIENT AMPHIBIAN

### BY JONI PHELPS HUNT

LONDON TOWN PRESS

The London Town *Wild Life* Series
Series Editor
Vicki León

*A Chorus of Frogs*
Principal photographer
Michael Fogden

Additional photographers
A. Cosmos Blank; John Cancalosi; Stephen Dalton; Jeff Foott;
Stephen J. Krasemann; Alex Kerstitch;  Kevin Schafer and
Martha Hill; Kennan Ward; T.A. Wiewandt; Doug Wechsler;
Art Wolfe; Belinda Wright; Norbert Wu

London Town Press
P.O. Box 585
Montrose, California  91021
www.LondonTownPress.com

Book design by Christy Hale
10  9  8  7  6  5  4  3  2  1

Printed in Singapore

Distributed by Publishers Group West

Publisher's Cataloging-in-Publication Data
Hunt, Joni Phelps.
A chorus of frogs : the risky life of an ancient amphibian / Joni
Phelps Hunt ; photographs by Michael Fogden [et al.] —2nd
ed.
p.  cm. — (London Town wild life series)
Originally published: San Luis Obispo, CA : Blake Books
©1993.
Summary: Explores the physical characteristics, life cycles,
and behavior of frogs and toads through full-color photographs
and text.
Includes bibliographic references and index.
ISBN 0-9766134-1-7
1. Frogs—Juvenile literature.   2. Toads—Juvenile literature.
[1. Frogs. 2. Toads.] I. Fogden, Michael. II. Title. III. Series.
QL668.E2 H863  2005
597.8—dc22
2005930186

FRONT COVER: In the tropical rainforest lives the red-eyed
treefrog. A night hunter, its pupils open wide to find insects
in the dark.

TITLE PAGE: A red-eyed treefrog from Panama looks both ways,
thanks to its flexible eyeballs—a big help for a small frog that
wants to survive in a rainforest full of hungry creatures.

BACK COVER: The soft underside of this masked treefrog takes
up water through the porous skin. Toads absorb water in the
same way.

# Contents

# Wet or dry, they welcome spring

Our planet was once a world without song. Then the ancestors of today's frogs appeared on land, and began to vocalize. Long before the music of birds was heard, frogs began to sing choruses at dusk, and their lusty croaks came to welcome spring.

Herpetologists, the scientists who study frogs and toads, classify them as amphibians, the Greek word for double life. It's a fitting name. Frogs and toads are the only four-legged animals on earth that go through a metamorphosis. Born with gills in water, they change into air-breathing creatures with lungs. As adults, most of them can lead a double life in both wet and dry environments.

▶ The granular glass frog has paper-thin skin. Frogs use lungs to breathe, but also take oxygen from the air through their skins.

Because frogs and toads often live near us, in wetlands, gardens, and roadside ditches, we get a chance to see the way they change from eggs to tadpoles to adults, in one of the most magical transformations in the animal kingdom.

Touch a frog, and you'll notice it has no fur, feathers, or scales to protect it. The skin of frogs feels cold, smooth, and slick. Most toads feel cold, bumpy, and dry. But all species need water—and frogs and toads drink it through their skins, not their mouths.

Like other amphibians, including salamanders and newts, frogs are ectothermal creatures, whose body temperature goes up or down, depending on the temperature of their surroundings.

This cold-blooded nature doesn't stop frogs from living almost everywhere in

▼ Frogs and toads belong to the scientific order called Anura, or tailless ones. Main points of difference between them:

► A strawberry poison dart frog, also nicknamed the blue jeans frog, sits on a huge leaf and takes in water through its skin.

the world. Over 4,700 species have been identified so far. Leopard frogs live in meadows and lakeshores. Bullfrogs croak in marshes and ponds. Wood frogs can be found north of the Arctic Circle, and remain frozen without injury for weeks. Spadefoot toads and Australian frogs burrow underground in the desert. In forests, treefrogs live high in the branches. In mountains, frogs and toads are happy at heights over 15,000 feet.

| KEY DIFFERENCES | |
| --- | --- |
| MOST FROGS | MOST TOADS |
| Have wet, smooth skin | Have dry, bumpy skin |
| Have streamlined bodies | Have heavy bodies |
| Move by making big leaps | Move by walking or making short hops |
| Live in fresh water or close to it | Live on land, further from fresh water |
| Flee danger by jumping away | At sign of danger, sit without moving |

▲ Sticky toes, quick reflexes, and good balance let this poison dart frog perch on the flimsiest—or thorniest—flower.

Tropical regions, moist and warm year-round, are natural homes to 80 percent of all frog species. Some occupy the rainforest floor or swamps, while others spend their lives among the trees.

Just as frog habitat varies greatly, so does size. The Cuban frog, smallest in the world, is lucky to reach half an inch long. But the chunky goliath frog of Africa can grow to a foot wide. Most adult frogs and toads, however, average two to five inches of body length.

Frogs are among the most harmless of all creatures on earth. Whenever frogs are thought of as pests, it is usually because

▼ Thanks to the suction power of its eighteen toe discs, the two-inch red-eyed treefrog moves easily around its rainforest home.

human beings have tried to manage wildlife by introducing non-native species. That was how the American bullfrog became the most invasive species in the western United States. In Australia, the notorious cane toad was brought to that continent to control a sugarcane beetle. Result: Australia is overrun with a poisonous breed of toad that squirts venom three feet and eats practically everything (including native frogs) except the pest for which it was imported.

But by nature, frogs are one of the world's most helpful animals. They may be the world's greatest gobblers of harmful pests, from mosquitoes to flies. They also play a key role in the food chain of life. Thousands of animals, from wading birds to alligators to raccoons, depend on frogs as a food source.

Frogs have lived on earth for 200 million years—about 80 times longer than we have. They've seen ice ages come and go, and survived mass extinctions of other species. But late in the 20th century, their populations around the world began to fall drastically. Several species have since vanished completely. Could the fate of these hardy, ancient creatures be a warning signal about the larger fate of our planet?

▲ The red-eyed tree frog sleeps by day, hiding its green skin among leaves. A hole in a leaf makes an excellent place to ambush insects.

# From tongues to toes

Frog eyes glow like jewels of berry red, orange, greenish-yellow, or gold. Besides being big, bulgy, and beautifully colored, each eye works independently, letting the frog see in a wide circle around itself. Frogs have color vision, and can spot predators up to ten feet away. When frogs swim underwater, they can raise and lower their eyes like periscopes. They also have see-through membranes that act as diving masks.

Below the eyes are two flat eardrums called tympanum. A bullfrog has ears twice the size of its big eyes. Frogs can also hear underwater. Keen hearing is important at mating time, when female frogs follow the calls of the males of their species to the breeding pond.

◄ By day, the Couch's spadefoot toad drowses underground in its prairie and desert habitats. At night, its huge eyes have excellent vision.

Sometimes frogs appear to be all mouth. But they need it: they can't chew and must swallow their prey alive and whole—not an easy job when it's a squirming mouse or jittery grasshopper.

Most frogs have small front teeth, useful only to keep its meal from crawling back out. To stuff its prey down, the frog lowers its eyes into the roof of its mouth.

Inside that froggie grin is a secret weapon: a sticky-tipped tongue attached at the front, that darts out and back in less than a second, faster than your eye can see.

A male frog or toad is designed to make noise. As air crosses its vocal cords, it vibrates, producing sound. Air also inflates the vocal sac, increasing the croak output. Some males vocalize alone to warn other males or claim territory. For breeding, groups of males form choruses to attract mates. Some female species are able to vocalize as well. Since they have no vocal sacs, their voices are soft.

What do frogs and toads sound like? Most of us are familiar with the Pacific treefrog and other species that make a sound like, "ribbit, ribbit." But many frogs

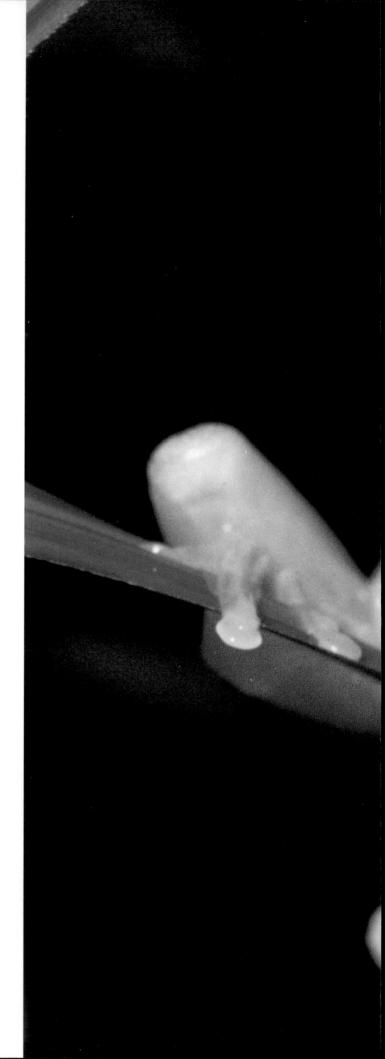

► Males of almost every species vocalize. This yellow treefrog of Costa Rica has a vocal sac beneath its throat to make its call resonate. Frog song has even more variety than birdsong.

make music. Spring peepers give melodious calls. The American toad utters a long high-pitched trill. Frogs in chorus come up with odd sound effects, too. Toads purr, buzz, bellow, or make car-honk noises; some frogs sound like creaking doors or whistles. And they do all this with their mouths closed!

Frogs open their mouths to vocalize only if a predator grabs them—then they give a loud squawk or distress call.

It's quite a sight to see males in mid-song. Frogs with one vocal sac appear to be blowing the world's biggest chewing gum bubble. Males with double vocal sacs look like they are wearing water wings.

Even when a frog isn't singing, its throat moves constantly, to get oxygen into its lungs. To help the lungs supply oxygen throughout its body, these animals also absorb oxygen through their skin. Because their skin dries out easily, frogs keep it moist with special mucus-producing glands, making their skin feel slippery. Dry skin can be deadly because it won't allow oxygen to pass through.

◄ A red-eyed treefrog begins a giant leap, trying to score a direct hit on a cricket.

Frogs don't drink water. While swimming or sitting in puddles, frogs soak up all they need.

As they grow into adults, frogs shed too-tight skins regularly. Once grown, frogs continue to shed their old skin for a new one about once a week. Nothing is wasted in a frog's world; they usually eat the discarded skin.

Frogs and toads have backbones but no ribs, and feel like beanbags when picked up. Toads tend to be fat and chunky. Frogs often have slender bodies, but can be plump as well. The hind legs of frogs are pure muscle, and are as long as the entire body. When they spring into action, they can make a direct hit on prey or enter the water as neatly as a diver. Although toad legs are shorter and weaker, they walk well and can hop steadily for quite a distance.

On each hind foot, frogs have five strong webbed toes that let them swim with ease. Many terrestrial frogs and toads dig in the dirt and have modifications to help, such as the spurs on spadefoot toads. Treefrog species have less need for webbing. Instead, they possess long toe discs that curl like fingers around branches and stick like suction cups to leaves.

▲ A frog's tongue is long and attached at the front of its mouth. The tip is sticky, making it a terrific weapon.

Frogs are always ready for a meal. As far as a frog is concerned, if it moves, and it's smaller—grab it! Menu items include: worms, mayflies, slugs, snails, beetles, roaches, grasshoppers, spiders, grubs, mosquitoes, flies, and larvae found in water. They aren't fussy eaters—but no poisonous hairy caterpillars, please. Frogs also dine on eggs, tadpoles, smaller frogs—and their own dead skin whenever they molt. Larger species with strong jaws, like the horned frogs, also hunt snakes, baby turtles, mice, and fishes.

Earthbound frogs move in for the kill in various ways. Some toads crawl. Other frogs stalk almost on tiptoe. British natterjack toads run in quick bursts on their short back legs.

In or near the water, most amphibians use the ambush method: remaining still and waiting for prey to come to them.

To keep alive in a frog's world, however, you've got to keep moving. These small animals have many enemies, few weapons, and little body strength to defend themselves when confronted. A frog's must-avoid list includes: snakes, skunks, turtles, hawks,

▼ A masked treefrog clings to a rainforest flower, waiting for mosquitoes to buzz by. Snap! Faster than your eye can follow, the frog's tongue grabs its prey.

wading birds, mink, foxes, raccoons, hedgehogs, wolves, otters, bats, rats, and domestic cats.

Frogs have survived because they are experts at fleeing. A common bullfrog can jump 20 times its own body length. Some tiny frog species soar as much as 40 times their own length.

To get away from predators, treefrog species glide 100 times their body length. Generous webbing between the toes acts as their parachute. In Asia and the South Pacific, species like the flying frog and the larger gliding frog easily sail from tree to tree.

At times, these amphibians rely on startle tactics. Some frogs give a jump and a hideous scream, called a distress call,

▶ It can be a frog-eat-frog world, when an ornate horned frog gobbles a spadefoot toad. A wide mouth comes in handy to swallow prey whole.

▼ Rain frogs have many enemies—like the rear-fanged snake. Many creatures, from snakes to mammals, depend on frogs as a food source.

when touched by an attacker, at times discouraging it.

The European toad and the crucifix toad of Australia use another trick. When threatened by a snake, they swell up, stand on tiptoe, and tower over it. Sometimes the snake decides its prey is too much a mouthful, and leaves.

The four-eyed frog of Chile startles in a different way. When danger nears, it lifts its rear end and flashes two huge eyespots on its rump at the surprised predator.

When frightened, frogs sometimes play dead, entering a state of unconsciousness. If the predator leaves, the frog soon recovers and hops away.

Camouflage and cryptic or protective coloration are other ways that frogs keep from being eaten. The Surinam toad does an uncanny imitation of a weed. The gray treefrog wears a pattern that blends with the lichens on the treetrunks to which it clings. Other toads and frogs disguise themselves as dead leaves, moss, or mud. In its sandy burrow, the midwife toad makes a perfect match.

▲ The horned frog of Peru makes a threat display and opens its mouth to give a distress call, a scream that often startles its attacker.

◄ A Pacific treefrog has pigment cells that let it change color. When it's cold, it can darken its skin to absorb more heat. On sunny days, the frog can lighten itself in ten minutes to reflect the sun's rays off its body. Color changes help it hide from enemies, too.

Frogs and toads are masters at imitating glossy green leaves, bark, lily pads, bulrushes, and even colorful plants. Some species can change color, thanks to special pigment cells called chromatophores. They allow some frogs to turn pale, others darker, when fearful, excited, too hot, or too cold. In the midday sun of Africa, one green frog is able to turn white to reflect heat. Another African species lives on the arum swamp lily. When it's in bloom, the arum frog is white to match the flowers; when they turn brown, the frog turns brown also.

Frogs also live longer by wearing flash or startle coloration. The fire-bellied and the yellow-bellied toads have green, brown, or gray backs. When threatened, they contort their bodies to show their underbellies, bright with red, orange, and yellow warning colors.

A few frog species use mimicry, copying the colors or patterns of dangerous or poisonous species to give the impression that they too are toxic.

◀ This Pacific treefrog rests on fungus growing from a tree trunk. Abundant in the western states, these frogs spend time in trees but also live in marshes, grasslands, and near mountain streams. The Pacific treefrog's "ribbit, ribbit" call is famous and is often used for sound effects on television and in movies.

▼ A native of Ecuador and Colombia, the harlequin poison dart frog is shorter than your little finger. Although it mimics the plant it sits on, the frog's coloring warns it is poisonous and so it has no need to hide.

► Predators see the yellow polka-dots on this harlequin poison dart frog and steer clear. These small frogs hunt ants, mites, and beetles while the sun is up.

▲ In South American rainforests, the yellow-banded poison dart frog prowls the floor, foraging for beetles, ants, and termites.

Finally, there are the 175 species of frogs known as poison dart or poison arrow frogs. These most beautiful and deadly members of the frog family earned their name because rainforest tribes traditionally used their venom to make poison darts for their blowguns.

In daylight, while other frogs hide, these creatures fearlessly vocalize, wrestle each other over territory, and hop about, flashing neon colors, stripes, and polka-dots. Scientists refer to this coloration as aposematic or warning colors. (Other creatures, like the marine slug called a nudibranch, use them too.)

Rainbow-bright colors tell predators, "Back off—I am toxic!" Even at an inch or two long, each frog carries enough poison in its skin to paralyze a small animal. Three species are especially lethal. The golden poison dart frog carries enough toxin in its skin to kill a score of human beings.

Research has shown that young poison dart frogs eat certain insects that produce the skin toxins. Tadpoles and froglets lack the poison, and are therefore guarded by adult frogs until they mature.

Since many toad species have poison glands in their skin, you'd think they would have few enemies. Predators, however, such as snakes, have developed their own immunity to toad toxin. Or they have figured out ways to get around it. Shorebirds, skunks, and raccoons, for example, flip toads over to get at the unprotected belly.

# Let's go to the hop

▼ The short-headed frog of India has two vocal sacs. This one has joined a chorus of males, singing to win a mate. The males in some species have one vocal sac.

The frog and toad mating game has countless variations. In temperate climates, breeding usually occurs in spring. In dry climates, mating coincides with seasonal rainfall. In the tropics, there is nearly continuous breeding, and frogs mate several times a year. In climates with hot summers and cold winters, species use different strategies. Leopard frogs and spring peepers tolerate very cold water, and breed at the first sign of spring. Mink frogs reproduce later, when summer has warmed the water. That means their tadpoles must overwinter beneath the pond ice and make their change into froglets the

◄ Small but ornery, two males tussle over territory. Fights like this one between strawberry poison dart frogs may last an hour or more. Poison dart males also do combat over female frogs.

next summer. Species like the American toad breed late but lay huge amounts of eggs, which turn into tadpoles very fast.

While most eggs are laid in water, some are laid on land, or even in trees. Frog species that breed in water often return each year to the same pond or area—a behavior called site fidelity.

In places with cold winters, many species go dormant, digging burrows underground or underwater. When spring and warmer weather arrives, frogs come out of hibernation. Their first urge is return to the waters of their original home to breed. Many species have to migrate to do so.

Golden toads once gathered in excited groups like this one,
when rains filled their breeding pools of Monteverde Cloud Forest
Reserve in Costa Rica. Hundred of bright orange-colored males sang
to the larger, darker females before mating. Golden toads have not
been seen in years and the species is thought to be extinct.

Male frogs reach the pond first, migrating after dark in small groups. Toads hop to it both day and night. Some toads migrate as much as nine miles. In Great Britain, toads move in large groups. During migration, even obstacles like walls and roads do not deter. To keep frog and toad road-kill to a minimum, human volunteers in some countries dig tunnels under roads or use toad buckets to ferry animals to the other side.

Once at the breeding area, males gather to bellow in groups, beginning at dusk and into the night. Many ponds are chosen because they are small and free of fishes. They soon become crowded with more than one species.

Each species launches a different call, often two notes or a short single note, repeated quickly. Some male choruses are a series of croaks; others are sweet, such as the bell-like tones of the green treefrog. Certain species resemble dogs barking, pigs grunting, or chickens clucking. Even stranger are the males whose best efforts sound like snores, banjos, foghorns, or farm machinery. Choruses can be heard as much as a mile away.

Heavy with eggs, the females arrive. In the din, each sharp-eared female somehow locates the male chorus of her own species. Often there are five to ten male frogs for every female. The voice that wins a female may be the one that sings faster and longer. Or it may that larger males with deeper voices win more mates. So far, these amphibians aren't telling.

Most activity takes place in the dark, often leading to confusion and mistaken

▶ The golden toad male hugs a female in mating behavior called amplexus. This causes the female to release her eggs into the water, where the male fertilizes them.

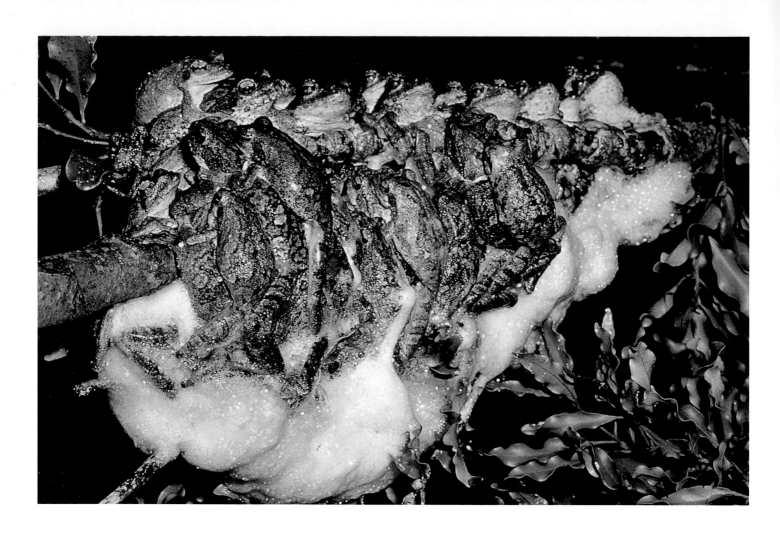

▲ Gray foam-nest treefrogs gather on a branch above an African pond to breed. After females secrete mucus, males thrash their hind legs to whip it into a stiff, foamy nest.

▼ A cat-eyed snake in the rainforest helps itself to eggs from a red-eyed leaf frog. Since many frog eggs don't survive, some female species lay them by the thousands.

◄ When the tadpoles of the gray foam-nest frog hatch, they wiggle to make a hole to get out.

identity. Several males may clasp the same female, and end up fighting. A male frog may grab another male, or a female of another species. The one being grabbed quickly indicates there's a problem by making a release call, a series of low clicking noises.

Among some toad species, the female makes the choice by nudging her selection. Most of the time, the male does the choosing. He hops onto the female's back, clasping her under the armpits or around her middle. This tight grip is called amplexus and may last for hours—even days.

Once in his grip, the female may hop off in search of a better breeding site, with her mate getting a free ride. When she's found the right place, the female frog begins laying eggs in water. Frogs lay between one and 35,000 eggs; most species lay several thousand. Out of that number, the odds are that only two to five will survive to become frogs.

As the female lays, the male adds sperm to fertilize them. Water expands the jelly-like substance around the eggs, keeping them moist and somewhat protected.

Other species lay eggs on land. Several species of tropical treefrogs use leaves hanging over streams. Humid conditions keep the eggs from drying out while tadpoles develop inside. In two weeks or so, tadpoles break through the egg membrane, fall into the water, and begin their new lives.

A South American male leaf frog begins calling during rainstorms. Once he finds a female, she carries him down the tree to a pond formed by the rain. She goes back up the tree to lay her eggs on a leaf above the water, and the male fertilizes them. The hard-working pair repeat the process, including trips to the pond to moisten the eggs, three to five times.

In other parts of the world, frogs build nests of mud or foam. In China, the fairy musician frog selects a site above a small pond, where the male digs a mud nest with his snout. He then gives a flutelike call to attract a mate. The female lays about 100 eggs in watery jelly. Rain soon washes the young into the pond to finish growing.

The male smith frog of Brazil makes a mud nest by hopping in a big circle, patting walls into place with his front feet. Once finished, the male begins his trademark call, which sounds like a blacksmith's hammer. After a brief courtship, eggs are laid in the nest, walled away from predators. Smith frog nests are built close together, leading to fights over territory. Males dunk foes, leg wrestle, and stab each other with bony spines on their front feet.

Some frogs, like the pig-nosed frog of Africa, build burrows. Near a pond, the female digs with her snout, stops to find a mate, then finishes the burrow with the male clasped to her back. After eggs are laid and fertilized, the male leaves. When tadpoles hatch in a few weeks, the tireless mother digs a tunnel to water, and the young wriggle to the pond.

In northern Mexico and the southwest United States, the Couch's spadefoot toad spends most of its life underground, sometimes in a state of hot-weather dormancy known as estivation. The sound of thunder lures it out of its burrow with the promise of a summer rainstorm heavy enough to form large pools. Soon a chorus of males attracts females, and eggs are laid that night. Eggs hatch in two to three days. Spadefoot tadpoles eat anything. Food is scarce, and they must grow quickly before their pool evaporates. When the pool is almost dry, tadpoles cluster together and wiggle their tails to squeeze more water out of the mud. The cycle from egg to spadefoot toadlet takes between nine days and three weeks.

Like the spadefoot, the water-reservoir frog of Australia lives many months underground and comes out during heavy rains to breed. As its name suggests, this

► Egg development can be a race against time. The eggs of the plains spadefoot toad must develop quickly before their pool evaporates—or a hungry tadpole eats them.

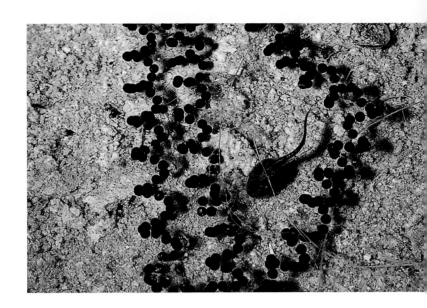

frog stores rainwater in its body while dormant. Aborigines, the indigenous people of Australia, often dig this frog out of its burrow for needed water.

When providing for their young, frogs make full use of natural resources. Damp moss near mountain streams works well for some Australian species. In Africa, one frog squeezes itself into broken bamboo to lay its eggs. Later, its tadpoles are well positioned to eat insects, other frogs' eggs, and plants.

In the rainforests of Central and South America, poison dart frogs rub noses and do a mating dance before the female lays up to a dozen eggs under a leaf or log. When tadpoles emerge, they wiggle onto the backs of mom or pop, and are carried aloft to the watery cups of bromeliad plants. Several poison dart species, including the harlequin frog, produce tadpoles that require a diet of unfertilized eggs. Females oblige by visiting the bromeliad ponds, and laying eggs for their tads.

Treefrogs also climb high on tree limbs to deposit eggs in these miniature ponds, sometimes adding a substance that thickens the water and reduces evaporation.

Most frog and toad parents lay and fertilize eggs, then let nature take its course. Some, however, stick around to help their young survive—perhaps as many as one out of ten species.

A glass frog species that makes its home in mountain streams of Costa Rica is one. The male babysits the eggs, clustered on a leaf, and keeps them moist with water from his bladder. The barking frog of Texas performs a similar service for offspring.

In the river basins of South America lives a beady-eyed, utterly alien-looking creature called the Surinam toad. A bottom dweller that never leaves murky water, it hunts prey by feel, using sensing organs on its spidery, whitish-brown toes. It has no vocal cords or tongue and inhales its food.

Mating begins when the male Surinam toad attracts a mate underwater by making clicking noises. While the pair swims around, the male clinging to the female, the skin on her back swells. They swim to the surface and somersault back into the river. During the descent, the female

▶ Both male and female poison dart frogs tote their tadpoles to small ponds for safety. But first the tads have to wiggle onto the sticky back of one parent.

releases eggs which the male fertilizes and pushes into her swollen skin. For hours, they continue the somersault routine until 50 to 100 eggs are stuck into the female's flat back. In days, her skin grows to cover the eggs. As they develop, the mother goes about her underwater life. After a three to four-month incubation, fully formed little frogs pop from her back.

Some treefrogs use waterless methods to incubate their eggs. The female leaflike marsupial frog carries her young in a pouch on her back until fully formed froglets emerge—without ever being in

▶ The female of the pygmy marsupial frog species carries six or seven large eggs in a pouch on her back. When her tadpoles are ready, she goes to a pool or a water-filled bromeliad plant, opens her pouch, and puts them into their new home.

▼ The rain frog of the Costa Rican cloud forest lays large transparent eggs on moss or damp leaves. Each holds enough yolk food for the young as it becomes a tadpole, then a froglet. When it's time, the froglet uses a horny spike on its nose to cut itself free.

water. In another marsupial frog species, the male guards the eggs, located in a nest on the ground. When they hatch, the male gets egg jelly all over himself. Attracted to this goo, some of the tadpoles swim to him and slide into his pouches, where they later emerge as new frogs.

In the forests of southern Chile and Argentina, the female Darwin's frog lays 20 to 30 eggs in damp moss or leaf litter and goes away. Several males guard the eggs until the tadpoles begin to move. One or more of the males scoops up eggs with his tongue and swallows them. They fall through slits into his vocal sac, where they remain for 50 days until grown. When the male frog opens his mouth, out slither tiny miniatures of him.

In the Australian rainforest, an unusual parenting event used to take place among gastric brooding frogs, now thought to be extinct. The female swallowed some of her own eggs, which grew in her stomach. The eggs developed into tadpoles and were born, one by one, on the tongue of the female. Researchers still don't know how she did this without digesting the babies with her stomach acid.

After mating on land, the male midwife toad of western Europe entwines a string of 20 to 60 eggs around his legs. To protect them, he hides during the day. At night he looks for food and dampens the eggs with dew. About a month later, when the eggs are ready to hatch, the male dips his legs into shallow water and the tadpoles swim off.

Only two species, a West African toad and a Puerto Rican frog, give birth to live offspring. Two froglets or toadlets are born per litter. Although parents don't lose eggs or tadpoles to predators, the same dangers still await the young frogs or toads. Live birth may not be an efficient way for amphibians to reproduce.

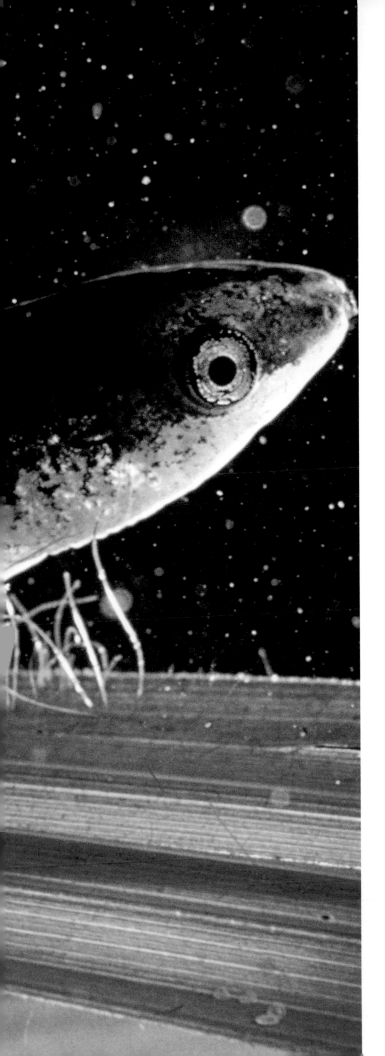

# Transforming from tadpoles

*A*fter hatching from an egg, a fishlike creature living in water turns into a land animal with lungs, four legs, and no tail. Although it seems as unlikely as kissing a frog and taking home a prince, it happens all the time. This process, by which a tadpole grows and changes shape to a frog, is called metamorphosis.

The time it takes varies by species. When frog eggs are laid in water, the top part is alive and growing. The yolk at the bottom supplies food. In half a day, the nervous system takes shape. Gills start to show,

◄ In the watery world of a pond or puddle, a tadpole roots in the mud for decaying matter and hunts small animals called protozoa. The tadpole also eats plant algae—the only time in its life it will eat its vegetables.

▼ These are tadpoles of the leopard frog. The one with front and hind legs will become a froglet sooner. A froglet with a tail faces special dangers. It can no longer swim as well as a tadpole, but still can't jump as well as a frog.

a tail bud grows, and a mouth forms. In a day or two, the embryo hatches from the egg jelly and hangs by its mouth.

Soon the heart beats, blood runs through gills, and eyes develop. When blood circulates in the tail a day later, the brown or black animal looks like a tadpole. At four days, skin covers its feathery gills. It can swim, eat algae, and hunt down protozoa.

Most eggs hatch into tadpoles in three to 25 days.

New tadpoles face many dangers. Animals that enjoy tadpoles for dinner include: water beetles, dragonfly nymphs, water scorpions, fishes, ducks, wading birds, spiders, and snakes. Some tadpoles, such as those of the meadow treefrog and the spadefoot toad, also eat frog eggs

▼ Juicy, plump, and red as its namesake, this highly endangered tomato frog comes from the island of Madagascar.

▲ Often called the smiley frog for its friendly appearance, White's treefrog is a common sight in Australian ponds, rainwater tanks, and farm buildings.

and their fellow tadpoles.

Besides facing the dangers of being eaten, tadpoles compete with thousands of others for food. Diseases and water mold can kill tadpoles. Heat or drought can dry up a pond. Or the reverse can happen, when heavy rains fill ponds with mud, burying the food supply.

The final change from tadpole to frog is rapid. Land species change faster than those that live in water all the time; desert dwellers are quicker yet. The leopard frog makes its leap from tadpole to froglet in three days.

Telltale signs show that metamorphosis has begun. Small hind legs appear on the tadpole. Then front legs. The tail grows shorter, gradually absorbed by the body as food. Gills disappear, and lungs develop.

Now a froglet, the animal has a much larger mouth, bulging eyes, and a working tongue. Instead of eating plants, it catches flies and crunches beetles. The skin toughens, adult coloring appears, and the froglet's legs get long and muscular.

After metamorphosis, a frog grows rapidly for about two years. As a full-sized adult, it will be about ten times the size it was as a froglet.

How long do frogs live? Even herpetologists have to make best guesses. In captivity, frogs and toads can live to 20 years or more. In the wild, lifespans are known to be as short as four months for the cricket frog, and perhaps a few years for most other species.

▲ A North American leopard frog shows off its leaping ability. Once common, this species has become rare.

In ancient cultures, from Egyptian to Mayan, frogs were often worshipped. By medieval times, however, people saw frogs and toads as evil creatures associated with enchantment. In the 20th century, modern society viewed frogs as cartoon characters.

Today frogs are recognized as bio-indicators, as creatures that can tell us whether our air, our water, and our planet are healthy. And they are in peril.

Because of their porous skin and need for water, these animals get directly exposed to countless substances in the environment. Since the 1980s, frog and toad populations have disappeared faster than a leopard frog can leap. Dozens of species have vanished, from the golden toads of Costa Rica to the gastric brooding frogs of Australia. Once-common species, like the leopard frog in Canada, have become rare. Just as troubling, mass deformities of young frogs have occurred on four continents and in 46 states.

Natural fluctuations in population cannot account for these losses. Frogs are even disappearing in areas established to protect them. California's Yosemite National Park has lost three of its seven native species. In 2004, a global assessment by 500 scientists in 60 countries showed that one-third of all amphibian species are threatened with extinction.

What has brought the ancient and successful frog family to this point? Habitat loss, for one. When human beings drain ponds and wetlands for development, clear-cut rainforests for timber or mining, and remove hedgerows and wilderness areas, frogs have nowhere to go.

Pollution is another factor. Smog, pesticides, and metals give frogs a triple whammy, poisoning air, breeding grounds, and waterways. Acid rain and snow taint water and soils.

Climate change, from El Nino patterns to ozone layer thinning, is a third factor. Any increase in ultraviolet radiation causes cell mutations in frogs, deformities, and death. Species that breed at high altitudes are most at risk. The golden toad may be the first creature whose extinction can be directly linked to global warming.

Hard hit by a combination of these and other factors, frog and toad populations fall prey to more parasites, viruses, and fungal diseases.

The future of our small, wetsuited friends looks grim. But there are signs of hope.

Frogs were once used in great numbers for dissections in the United States. Today, ethical concerns about overharvesting have changed priorities. Countries that once killed vast quantities of frogs for the food trade have found that frogs are more valuable alive and eating mosquitoes, than

▲ A North American marsh contains many bullfrogs like this one. Habitat loss, especially of wetlands and rainforests, is the biggest problem facing frog populations worldwide.

dead on a plate. More and more governments are banning the use of herbicides near water.

Thanks to media attention about extinctions and frog deformations, and easier access via the internet, a growing body of activists now exist, from schoolkids to farmers to seniors. Helping alliances, from frog survey groups to websites offering educational programs, have linked up worldwide.

Scientists have always prized frogs for contributions they have made to research on cancer, muscle regeneration, and the immune system. From toxins of now endangered frogs has come epibatidine, a painkiller 200 times more potent than morphine, and other medical applications. As individuals, we need to make the world more frog-friendly. We can start by

▲ Glass frogs of Central America have see-through skin. On this bare-hearted glass frog, its stomach and other organs are visible.

preserving their pocket habitats, or creating new ones, from ponds and gardens to patches of woods. This approach has won much support in Great Britain. Instead of buying pet frogs, feed toads on their own turf, or watch tadpoles grow and change in their home ponds. We all have a stake in what happens. What a poor world it would be, without the signs of frogs and their sounds of life each spring.

# Secrets of frogs

- Frogs need water but don't drink it—they soak it up through their thin skins.

- Toads have poisonous skin glands—but few can do any harm to human beings. Warts? That's just a myth.

- Frogs wear bright colors to send a message: "Hello, I'm poisonous!" Toxin from one tiny golden poison dart frog could kill a score of monkeys—or people.

- Female frogs have no vocal sacs and rarely make a peep.

- Frogs have teeth, but don't use them to chew. Teeth keep live prey from wiggling out of a frog's mouth.

- How far can frogs jump? Bullfrogs have made winning leaps of 22 feet. Another champ is the rocket frog. It can soar 50 times the length of its body.

- In the deserts of Australia, aborigine tribes find fresh water in the body of a burrowing frog that stores it.

- To outwit predators, some frogs stand on tiptoe, others give a shrill scream, and others play dead.

- Many rainforest frogs never touch the ground. Living high in trees, they move by gliding from branch to branch.

- Diving flippers for human beings were copied from nature's perfect design: the webbed, five-toed back feet of a frog.

# Glossary

Alga/algae. Small, primitive plants, living mostly in water, which serve as an important food for tadpoles.

Amplexus. The tight grip of a male frog or toad on the body of the female during mating. Amplexus stimulates the release of her eggs.

Aposematic coloration. Bright warning colors, worn on the skin of poisonous frogs.

Bio-indicator species. Key groups, such as frogs, whose importance and direct exposure to the environment make them living monitors of planetary health.

Bromeliad. A rainforest plant, often with a cuplike center that holds water, serving as nursery to frog eggs and tadpoles.

Chromatophores. Specialized pigment cells in the skin of frogs, allowing them to change color.

Cryptic coloration. A way to hide from predators by wearing colors or camouflage that blends into the surroundings.

Distress call. A loud cry uttered by frogs and toads to evade or startle predators.

Dormant/dormancy. A state of greatly reduced activity and body function, entered by frogs during periods of heat, drought, or cold. Summer dormancy is called estivation. Winter dormancy is called hibernation.

Ectothermal. An animal's dependence on an outside heat source to raise or lower its body temperature; also known as "cold-blooded."

Extinction. The loss of an entire animal or plant population from the wild.

Herpetologist. A scientist who studies reptiles and amphibians, such as frogs and toads.

Indigenous people. The original human inhabitants of an area or region.

Invasive species. Non-native species that weaken or wipe out native species.

Metamorphosis. The change from one form to another, as in the three stages of frog and toad development: egg, tadpole, and adult.

Mimicry. The ability of one species to mimic or copy a more dangerous or toxic species to escape predators.

Molt. To shed skin and replace with new skin. Frogs do this regularly, as they grow.

Protozoan/protozoa. Tiny water-borne animals. With algae, an important food for tadpoles.

Site fidelity. The ability of frogs and toads to return to the same breeding grounds or ponds, year after year.

Terrestrial. Ground dwelling.

Toxic/toxins. Poisonous or harmful; poisons.

Tympanum. A flat, circle-shaped eardrum that allows frogs to hear underwater also.

Vocal sac. A pouch under the throat of a male frog or toad, used by the animal to help send its vocalizations.

◄ The golden mantella lives on the island of Madagascar. Mantella species come in many brilliant colors, not just orange. Admire but don't touch—their skins secrete poison.

### About the author
Award-winning nature book author Joni Hunt has also written other books for the London Town Wild Life series, including *A Shimmer of Butterflies, A Band of Bears, Secrets of the Desert,* and *A Swarm of Insects.*

### Photographers
Fifteen of the world's best contributed to this book. Principal photographer Michael Fogden supplied 17 superb photos. The red-eyed treefrog on the front cover was shot by Norbert Wu; the back cover was by Kevin Schafer/Martha Hill. A. Cosmos Blank/Photo Researchers, p. 16; John Cancalosi/DRK, p. 17 bottom; John Cancalosi, p. 40; Stephen Dalton/Photo Researchers, pp 14-15, 42; Michael Fogden/DRK, pp 4-5, 9, 10, 12-13, 18, 19 top, 24, 26-27, 29, 30 top & bottom, 31, 35 top & bottom, 36, 38-39, 44; Jeff Foott, p. 33; Stephen J. Krasemann/DRK, pp 7, 22; Alex Kerstitch, p.1; Kevin Schafer and Martha Hill, pp 17 top, 41 top, back cover; Kennan Ward, p. 19 bottom; T.A. Wiewandt/DRK, p. 10; Doug Wechsler, p. 43; Art Wolfe, pp 8, 20, 21, 23, 41 bottom, 46, 47; Belinda Wright/DRK, p. 25; Norbert Wu, front cover.

### Special thanks
- Dr. David C. Cannatella, University of Texas at Austin
- Linda Countryman, Docent, Los Angeles Zoo
- Harvey Fischer, Curator of Reptiles, Los Angeles Zoo
- Sue Schafer, Assistant Reptile Curator, San Diego Zoo
- Paige Torres Chamberlain

### Helpful organizations and websites
- Frogwatch USA, a project of National Wildlife Federation and the U.S. Geological Survey. Frog watching tips, field guides for local species, and volunteer opportunities to collect information about your local frog population. (www.nwf.org/frogwatchUSA)
- Global Amphibian Assessment. Amphibian diversity worldwide, with maps and information about number of species and threatened species, by country. (www.globalamphibians.org)
- Amphibian Conservation Alliance. Information-packed site with topical news, calls to action, and "froghoo!" links to amphibian biology, conservation, research, events, volunteer opportunities, educational resources for students and educators. (www.frogs.org)
- Amphibiaweb. Easy-to-use database of amphibians throughout the world. (www.amphibiaweb.org)
- National Biological Information Infrastructure (NBII), part of the U.S. Geological Survey. Examines various wildlife projects and issues with much information about frogs and amphibians. Includes worldwide teacher/student resources & website links. (www.nbii.gov/frog)
- Partners in Amphibian and Reptile Conservation (PARC) has a Student Partners (SPARC) program that offers regional species, project and event information. (www.parcplace.org/sparc)
- Earthwatch Institute. Science-based organization links scientists with volunteers to do research projects—many on frogs, toads, and habitats—in more than 50 countries. Results provide solid data for conservation groups and sustainability efforts. (www.earthwatch.org)
- The Exploratorium. San Francisco's most amazing museum has an equally valuable website, with lots of value-packed data and photos on frogs. (www.exploratorium.edu)

### To learn more
BOOKS & MAGAZINES
- *Amphibian Conservation.* Edited by Raymond D. Semlitsch. (Smithsonian Books 2003). A high-quality roundup of expert writing on threats to amphibians, disappearing populations and managing ecosystems.
- *Frogs* (WorldLife Library Series). By David Badger. (Voyageur Press 2000). Classy photos and conversational

► The loud colors of a blue poison dart frog say to predators, "Beware! I'm not good to eat." When frightened, it releases toxins from its skin.

text look at 50 species throughout the world and frogs' role in popular culture.

- *The Nature of Frogs: Amphibians with Attitude.* By Harry Parsons. (Greystone Books 2000). The title lives up to its promise; an excellent text by a herpetologist who can write, matched by closeup photos that jump off the page. Useful appendix of frog families.
- *Frogs & Toads of the World.* By Christopher Mattison. (Facts on File 2003). Another big book, heavily salted with photos.

VIDEOS, DVDs & CDs

- " Eyewitness—Amphibians." DK Publishing, 1995 VHS. Good footage amid silly filler about toads and witchcraft.
- "The Calls of Frogs and Toads." By Lang Elliott. Stackpole Books 2004. Book and CD. A 65-minute audio guide, covering a variety of calls by 42 eastern and central U.S. frogs and toads. Accompanied by an 80-page reference book on the science of amphibian calls.
- "Sounds of North American Frogs." By Charles Bogert. Smithsonian Folkways 1998. CD. Digitally remastered reissue of a 1959 recording of more than 75 U.S. species. Narrated by herpetologist Charles Bogert. A great teaching tool.

## Where to see frogs worldwide

- **Visit zoos and aquaria.** Most zoos, aquaria and natural history museums have frog exhibits or habitats from rainforest to wetlands to desert that house interesting and colorful species. Special exhibits feature specific types of frogs.

  Oustanding examples include the Hall of Reptiles and Amphibians at the American Museum of Natural History in New York; the National Aquarium in Baltimore; Atlanta Botanical Garden's amphibian conservation program; Audubon Aquarium of the Americas in New Orleans; Oregon Coast Aquarium; and the San Diego Zoo. For websites of zoos and aquariums and for details about ongoing or special exhibits in your geographical area or places you plan to visit, go to www. aza.org; select AZA Zoos & Aquariums and select by state or alphabetical order.

  In other parts of the world, zoos and aquaria feature frogs and other amphibians, often highlighting species native to their area.

- **Visit frog-friendly habitats within parks.** Thousands of local, state and national wildlife preserves, wildlife refuges, and wetlands sanctuaries offer close-up looks at frog species in their natural environments. Many are free.
- **Visit real rainforests.** The ones nearest the mainland United States are located in Hawaii, Costa Rica, Mexico, Guatemala, Belize, and Caribbean islands from Puerto Rico to Cuba. The money you spend as a visitor is a good way to encourage countries to save their natural resources, like frogs and rainforests.
- **Go on real-life scientific frog expeditions** through Earthwatch Institute (www.earthwatch.org). It has programs for kids 16 and up; scholarships and teacher programs, too.
- **Be a backyard frog explorer or create a haven for frogs in your backyard.** Once you know where to look and what to listen for, you'll spot local frogs with ease. Tips for setting up an area in your backyard or your school to welcome frogs and other wildlife are found at www.nwf.org/frogwatchUSA/ and www.audubon.org/bird/at_home/index.html. For those who live in Australia, frog-friendly gardening for local species is explored at www.frogs.org.au/frogwatch/friendly
- **Volunteer to count frogs.** National Wildlife Federation and the U.S. Geological Survey collect information about frog and toad populations throughout the United States. Anyone can volunteer; find out more information at www.nwf.org/frogwatchUSA.

# Index

Photographs are numbered in **boldface** and follow the print references after **PP** (photo page).